A LITTLE BOOK OF *life*

A LITTLE BOOK OF
life

RUSKIN BOND

RUPA
RAINLIGHT

Published in RAINLIGHT
by Rupa Publications India Pvt. Ltd 2012
7/16, Ansari Road, Daryaganj
New Delhi 110002

Sales Centres:
Allahabad Bengaluru Chennai
Hyderabad Jaipur Kathmandu
Kolkata Mumbai

Copyright © Ruskin Bond 2012

All rights reserved.
No part of this publication may be reproduced,
transmitted, or stored in a retrieval system, in any
form or by any means, electronic, mechanical,
photocopying, recording or otherwise, without the
prior permission of the publisher.

ISBN: 978-81-291-2009-0

Fourth impression 2015

10 9 8 7 6 5 4

The moral right of the author has been asserted.

Printed at Replika Press Pvt. Ltd, India

This book is sold subject to the condition that it
shall not, by way of trade or otherwise, be lent,
resold, hired out, or otherwise circulated, without the
publisher's prior consent, in any form of binding or
cover other than that in which it is published.

Introduction

As a schoolboy with literary inclinations, I read almost everything that came my way, from the plays of George Bernard Shaw to the thrillers of 'Bulldog Drummond', a forerunner of James Bond. A book that left a strong impression on me was a handsome volume called *Words to Live By*, in which various 'achievers' or people of eminence selected passages from the classics and various works of philosophy or religion. These passages or lines had inspired them at crucial moments, or during difficult periods of their lives.

This prompted me to keep my own little notebook or diary in which I put down the 'words of wisdom' that I came across in the books I read. Seventy years later, I am still doing it; as much out of habit as out of a need for advice from the great and the famous.

Well, there is always something to learn no matter how old we are, and I still turn to my little book in order to find words that might cheer me up when I am down in the dumps—as we all are, from time to time.

Perhaps you, dear reader, will find it helpful too. And I have asked my publisher to provide you with a few blank pages between sections, so that you can jot down your own thoughts, observations, or favourite quotes.

Keep this little book by your bedside, or on your desk, or on the kitchen shelf, and turn to it from time to time. It will have something comforting or helpful to say to you.

Ruskin Bond

Thank God for **beginnings** New years, new months— after every twenty-four hours, a new day, with the sun rising over a new world.

—Mrs George de Horne Vaizey

Believe in yourself.
Soon others will believe
in you too.

Love the beautiful,
desire the good, and do
your best.

·Ruskin Bond·

Study the face of nature
and you will never
be bored.

'Life can only be
understood backwards, but
it must be lived forwards.'
—*Søren Kierkegaard*

·A Little Book of Life·

'Reading is to the mind
what exercise is to the body.'
—*Joseph Addison*

'Never tell an unnecessary
lie. The truth has
great authority.'
—*P.D. James*

·Ruskin Bond·

Do not pray for an easy life.
Pray to be a stronger person.

Help a stranger in distress, and one day you will receive help when you least expect it.

·A Little Book of Life·

Most ideas never work—
unless you do.

'Light suppers make
long lives.'

—*Granny's kitchen proverb*

If you live for yourself
alone, you are in great
danger of being bored
to death.

'Never seek to tell thy love,
Love that never told can be;
For the gentle wind
does move
Silently, invisibly.'
—*William Blake*

We take it all for granted
when we are young—the
leaping, the running,
the loving, the fighting...

You have to be old before
you can appreciate
being young.
And then, of course,
you can only look back
on youth with a certain
wistfulness.

·Ruskin Bond·

Winston Churchill: 'We are all worms, but I do believe I am a glow-worm.'

By all means observe the conventions, but remember that it is only in personal independence that happiness is to be found. Stay free!

·A Little Book of Life·

The greatest victory is the one you win over yourself.

❧

Courtesy is a powerful weapon—the more so when it is used in the face of arrogance and hostility.

❧

·Ruskin Bond·

If you rest on your laurels,
you are wearing them in
the wrong place.

Grandmother defined a
true gentleman thus: 'He
must be gentle as a woman,
and manly as a man.'

Notes

'How shall we hoodwink them?'
asked the young demon in the old story.
Tell them there's plenty of time,
said the old demon of experience.
'Lots of time. They always fall for that.'

—Reverend P.B. Clayton

'Politics is the art by which politicians obtain campaign contributions from the rich and votes from the poor on the pretext of protecting each from the other.'
—*Oscar Ameringer*

He who is always trying, is doing; and he who is always doing, does.

Life will always give us what
we know we are worth.
It never fails to take us at
our own valuation.

Almost anyone can do the
first half of anything; only
the people who do the
second half arrive.

Adversity is always
intermittent; and therefore,
if effort is constant,
you are bound to win.

.26.

A Depression is a period
when people are obliged
to do without things their
forefathers never had.

·Ruskin Bond·

If you can smile when you feel hurt, the hurt is half cured.

Go and do things. You are bound to succeed in some of them.

·A Little Book of Life·

You will sometimes be punished when you do not deserve it. Before giving vent to your indignation, reflect on how often you have deserved punishment without receiving it.

And here's a good Arabic proverb: 'When your son grows up, make him your brother.'

Don't be depressed by your surroundings.
That pebble at your feet has as much beauty as any great work of art.

Praise all countries, but live in your own.

·A Little Book of Life·

If you want to travel fast,
keep to the old roads.

When too much work
accumulates, take a holiday.

·Ruskin Bond·

Travel is a pleasure only when I have no particular destination, and plenty of time in which to get there.

'When all men say you are an ass, it is time to bray.'
—*English proverb*

·A Little Book of Life·

Expect good, and good will come.

'Beware of all enterprises that require new clothes.'
—*Henry David Thoreau*

Most people are better than life allows them to be.

'If you have much, give of
your wealth.
If you have little, give of
your heart.'
—*Arabic proverb*

Notes

There is money to be made in
the **marketplace**
but under a shady tree
there is **rest.**

Your room must have
a window.
Look at the clouds, look
at the stars, look at the
good earth.

Step out lightly, step out
brightly, and luck will
come your way.

·Ruskin Bond·

When one man is indispensable, no man is free.

Sow an act, reap a habit.
Sow a habit, reap
a character.
Sow a character, reap
a destiny.

Be courageous. But if you don't have courage, have strong legs.

A great idea will always run faster than any censor.

·Ruskin Bond·

Avoid quarrels. You will find that most quarrels are weak on both sides.

'The turtle only makes progress when it sticks its neck out.'
—*James Bryan Conant*

Let no man take your
dream away.
It will sustain you to
the end.

Keep an open mind.
Different books, different
faiths, often say the
same thing.

·Ruskin Bond·

If we fear someone, we give
that person power over us.
Be gentle, but don't allow
yourself to be trod upon.

Don't let petty-minded
people prevent you from
doing your thing.
The dogs may bark but the
caravan moves on.

'Never measure your generosity by what you give, but rather by what you have left.'
—*Bishop Fulton J. Sheen*

Avoid long speeches. The less a man knows, the longer he takes to tell it.

If you have good health,
you are young;
and if you owe nothing,
you are rich.

Those who keep good
gardens are usually
contented folk. Always
make space for flowers,
even if all you have is a
window ledge.

·A Little Book of Life·

Be as interested as you possibly can in all things— and especially interested in some things.

'Nobody grows old merely by living a number of years.'
—*Samuel Ullman*

Failure is not defeat,
it is just learning
how to succeed.

If 100 per cent seems
impossible, let us achieve
the 95 per cent that
is possible.

·A Little Book of Life·

Notes

We have as much right to cry
as we have to laugh.
Men
given to tears
are
good men,
goes an old Greek saying.

One courageous thought will put to flight a host of troubles.

Something attempted may fail; inaction must fail.

·Ruskin Bond·

Believe in God.
Believe in people.
Believe in yourself.
Then go ahead!

'The strongest man in the world is the man who stands alone.'
—*Thomas H. Huxley*

Be true to yourself, and
you will be true to others.

To find happiness, look
halfway between too little
and too much.

·Ruskin Bond·

Don't give up. One success will erase many failures.

Try loving your enemies. If nothing else, you'll confuse them.

Think of others as if you were the others.

The difficult can be done immediately; the impossible takes a little longer.

·Ruskin Bond·

Stay still within, even if the world around you is all sound and fury.

Feeling down and out? Lift up your head and shout— 'It's a great day!'

·A Little Book of Life·

Now and then there comes a time in our affairs when courage is safer than prudence.

Be like water. There's no stopping it. No matter how tiny the trickle, it's going to get somewhere!

·Ruskin Bond·

It's of no great
consequence in this world
who lets you down, so long
as it isn't yourself.

How many dreams might
have become happy
realities but for that
terrible little sentence,
'Too much trouble!'

·A Little Book of Life·

When it pays better to talk
than to listen, change
your company.

To succeed in anything,
you have to care desperately
for the thing itself and not
for what it brings with it.

·Ruskin Bond·

What have we to expect?
Anything.
What have we to fear?
Nothing.
What have we to hope for?
Everything.

Most men want their children to be a credit to them. Wise men try to be a credit to their children.

·A Little Book of Life·

Notes

The sage lives in yesterday; the dreamer in tomorrow; the plodder in today. The successful man combines all these.

'Life may be short,' said Granny, 'but a smile is only a second's effort.'

May you have the wisdom
to be simple,
And the humour
to be happy!

·Ruskin Bond·

One of my favourite writers, John Buchan said, 'Trying to see something solid in the mist is the whole fun of life, and most of its poetry.'

Be honest, give your opinion for what it's worth; that is, if you are asked for it.

·A Little Book of Life·

'Good courage breaks bad luck.'
—*Proverb*

It is only through humility that we are able to preserve our dignity.

We have a lot to learn from children. A good teacher will always learn something from a good pupil.

The wisest man is he who doesn't think he is.

There are no fresh starts in life. But there are new directions.

'What is truly beautiful needs no adorning.'
—*Sataka*

Do what you know best,
and do it well.
Act impeccably. Everything
will then fall into place.

'Everything that depends
on others gives pain,
everything that depends on
oneself gives pleasure.'

—*Manu*

For any beauty you possess at sixteen, be very grateful. For the beauty you have at sixty, you may be proud—it is of your own achieving!

There is always a suitable work for every season, not to be done out of season. That is why we need not fear old age.

·Ruskin Bond·

'A lost battle is a battle one believes lost.'

—*Joseph de Maistre*

The great successes of the world have been the result of a second, a third, even a fiftieth attempt.

'Well begun is half done.'
Yes, but remember 'half done' is only half done.

When a difficulty presents
itself, remove it at once
if you can,
for the longer you look at it
the less you will like it.

·Ruskin Bond·

'If at times life seems a battle,' said Grandfather, 'well then, enjoy the battle. Make it a good battle.'

What if you failed yesterday? Today is not yesterday, is it?

Notes

They always come so quickly—
those **turning points**
in life—
and always down a lane
we are not watching.

'Live and let live' is a good maxim, but 'live and help live' is better.

The moment we can visualize possibilities, actualities are not very far away.

·Ruskin Bond·

'God gave us our faces,' said Granny, 'we give ourselves our expressions.'

The reason why few people succeed in moving mountains is that few of them practice on molehills.

'The torment of envy is
like a grain of sand
in the eye.'
—*Chinese proverb*

'What you think of yourself
is much more important
than what others
think of you.'
—*Seneca*

'A soft answer turneth away wrath; but a grievous word stirreth up anger.'
—*Proverbs 15:1*

If you can rule your own spirit, you are stronger than the man who rules a city.

·A Little Book of Life·

A picture on the wall is not just something to look at. After a time it becomes company.

'A merry heart doeth good like a medicine: but a broken spirit drieth the bones.'

— *Proverb 17:22*

·Ruskin Bond·

Value good friends.
Remember Coleridge's
words: 'Friendship is a
sheltering tree.'

Consider yourself dead that
you have completed your
life up to the present time;
then start living as though
your life has been gifted to
you again.

.85.

·A Little Book of Life·

Those who are overly religious are well-practised in self-deception.

❧

Every writer worth his salt suffers from a keen sense of failure, because he knows he could have done things better.
It's the bad writers who are always pleased with themselves.

❧

·Ruskin Bond·

Chart your own course
through life.
What the stars foretell is
strictly for astrologers.

In the spring the
mountains always look
as though they have
just been created.

·A Little Book of Life·

Notes

Progress

sometimes uses a comma,
but never a full stop.
Be useful, be wanted, be necessary.
There is no life for
those who aren't.

'Fanaticism consists in redoubling your efforts when you have forgotten your aim.'
—*George Santayana*

Egotism is really a failure of sympathy, a failure of proportion. To recognize this is the first step towards becoming a loving, just and well-balanced person.

·Ruskin Bond·

'No sacrifice is worth the name unless it is a joy. Sacrifice and a long face go ill together.'
—*M.K. Gandhi*

Be tranquil.
Do not plan life too early.
Follow your intuitions; take
gratefully the joys of life;
take its pains hopefully;
do your business cheerfully.
And leave the rest to God.

·A Little Book of Life·

There are some who go about proclaiming with complacent pride that they have no time to read or think. What then will they be able to give their children, apart from a fat cheque book?

'A thing is not necessarily true because a man dies for it.'
—*Oscar Wilde*

Grandfather said: 'If you cannot win, make the fellow ahead of you exert himself to the utmost.'

Written somewhere: 'We die only when the will dies.'

·A Little Book of Life·

'Nothing is at last sacred
but the integrity of your
own mind.'
—*Ralph Waldo Emerson*

'Destiny is simply the
strength of your desires.'
—*J. Garfield*

It is good that others
should succeed.
Do not allow their success
to cast a shadow on your
own efforts.

Before you get upset,
ask yourself:
Does it really matter?

Old age is not to be confused with growing old. We can grow old at any age—twenty-five, thirty, forty. And we can be young at seventy, seventy-five, eighty.

Never despair. But if you do, then work on in despair. There is always a light at the end of the tunnel.

·Ruskin Bond·

'The journey of a thousand miles begins with one step.'
—*Lao Tzu*

Friends for the table are
easy to find;
but rare are those when
danger is near.

·A Little Book of Life·

The trouble with rich people is that they never seem to have any cash in their pockets. Afraid of pickpockets?

'You know, the way love can change a fellow is truly frightful to contemplate.'
—*P.G. Wodehouse*

'Experience is the knowledge that enables you to recognize a mistake when you make it a second time.'
—*Franklin P. Jones*

Sympathy is what one woman offers another in exchange for details.

Notes

Have you noticed that both **the Sun and the Moon** look twice their natural size just when they are coming and when they are going? So it is with troubles.

'Whoever scorns the poor reviles his own Maker.'
—*Proverbs 17:5*

Nothing really ends happily ever after, but if you come to terms with your own isolation, then, paradoxically, it becomes immediately possible to find a friend.

·Ruskin Bond·

It is a human being's privilege to fashion his inner life for himself—without the interference of priests, pundits, popes, babas, and other peddlers of spirituality.

Don't complain too much. Things will come right by themselves.

·A Little Book of Life·

'It is impossible to enjoy idling thoroughly unless one has plenty of work to do.'
—*Jerome K. Jerome*

Wherever you go, most of your life will have to happen in your mind.

·Ruskin Bond·

Adversity is always
intermittent; and therefore,
if effort is constant,
you are bound to win.

If you visit your bean and
lettuce merchant
every day, you won't have
to visit your chemist.

·A Little Book of Life·

Be guarded in your speech.
Don't talk too much. Many
words invite many defeats.

Happiness: He who has
happy children is
greater than a king.

·Ruskin Bond·

'If death was a thing that money could buy,
The rich they would live, and the poor they would die.'
—J. Sheridan Le Fanu

Do what you feel you must do. Don't listen to other people. Let them go to the devil. It's your life, not theirs.

·A Little Book of Life·

'By doing nothing, one wins the world.
But when one grasps, the world is beyond winning.'
—*Lao Tzu*

To be successful, one has to pit one's wits not against people, but against life.

·Ruskin Bond·

What I valued, I lost;
What I gave, I gained.

Never be dismissive of
the young. Never be
contemptuous of the old.

'To handle yourself, use your head; to handle others, use your heart.'
—*Eleanor Roosevelt*

Do things at your own pace. And know when to stop!

Some people believe in a world where people do this or that because they are good or evil. In the real world people act because they have to.

'Money often costs too much.'
—*Ralph Waldo Emerson*

Notes

Happiness:
A cherry tree,
bowed down by the night's
heavy rain,
suddenly rights itself,
flinging pellets of
water in my face.

'There is no cure for birth and death save to enjoy the interval.'
—*George Santayana*

Anyone alive who wishes to preserve his sanity must first of all preserve his sense of humour. And then his sense of wonder.

There are no general truths. But there are particular truths: who did what, when, why. Especially why.

'Success is doing what you want to do, when you want, where you want, with whom you want, as much as you want.'
—*Anthony Robbins*

The trouble with marriage is that it sets you on a very predictable course.

In the long run, ability counts for more than personality. (As I depend on the former—for I am a realistic man—I should keep public appearances to the minimum!)

·Ruskin Bond·

Simplicity must never be confused with simple-mindedness.

'A great man is always willing to be little.'
—*Ralph Waldo Emerson*

'An old man loved is winter with flowers.'
—*Old German proverb*

One of life's greatest pleasures lies in watching a plant grow—from seed to seedling, to green branch to bough, to flower, to fruit.

·Ruskin Bond·

Life is not something to be put up with, but a gift to be enjoyed with zest.

🌿

'A mirror is brighter when
polished with grit.'
—*Amir Khusrau*

🌿

I wouldn't go so far as to say that a garden is the answer to all problems, but it's amazing how a little digging and friendly dialogue with the good earth can help reactivate us when we grow sluggish or morose.

'A strong man and a waterfall always channel their own path.'
—*Anonymous*

Each one of us is a mass of
imperfections, and to be
able to recognize and live
with our imperfections,
our basic natures, defects
of genes and birth, makes
for an easier transit
on life's journey.

You can generally get
success if you do not
want victory.

·A Little Book of Life·

Epicurus says, 'Death does not concern us.'
It is not something we live to experience—we cannot lose what cannot be missed.

❦

It's the simple things in life that keep us from going crazy: a pigeon in the skylight, sunshine, birdsong, the bedside book, the potted geranium...

❦

·Ruskin Bond·

After years of striving,
and finding and losing
and striving again, now,
past seventy, I think I have
learnt something of the
value of stillness;
I don't fret so much;
I laugh at myself more
often; I don't laugh at
others; I live life at my
own pace.
Is this wisdom, or is it
just old age?

Notes

Maxims from my grandmother's recipe book:
'Dry bread at home is better than roast meat abroad.'
Eating and drinking should not keep men from thinking.

One of the most effective forms of healing has been largely neglected by doctors and patients—that's healing by reading. If you are in the dumps or in bed with a bug, or recovering from a serious illness, or waiting for a fracture to heal, get hold of books by your favourite authors and read as much as you can. You will start feeling better far sooner than if you simply lie on your back and feel sorry for yourself. (If the books put you to sleep,

·Ruskin Bond·

all the better.) And it's safe, too: I have yet to hear of anyone dying from an overdose of reading.

Winners hang on when losers let go.

You will find life exactly as you take it, make it, live it, and give it.

Aim at a lovely simplification of life, and so give your soul room to grow.

·Ruskin Bond·

Bad times are good times
to prepare for better times.

If you are capable of
smiling, no one will bother
whether you are
good looking or not.

·A Little Book of Life·

'There is skill in all things,
even in making porridge.'
—*Granny's kitchen proverb*

'There is no dependence
that can be sure
but a dependence
upon one's self.'
—*John Gay*

The only truly educated
person is the self-educated.

To live in peace with
others, first make peace
with yourself.

'Your own friend, and your father's friend, forsake not; neither go into your brother's house in the day of your calamity: for better is a neighbour that is near than a brother far off.'
—*Proverbs 27:10*

Authors should be read, not heard.

Often, it isn't poverty that makes us poor, but the inability to cope with hardship. Life is as unfair as it is fair and fate is blind; only our ability to carry on, regardless, is our wealth and fortune.

A purpose is something to achieve, not talk about.

·A Little Book of Life·

'The beauty of life is nothing but this, that each should act in conformity with his nature and his business.'
—W. Somerset Maugham

'Let your neighbours discover you before you make yourself known to them.'
—Zen wisdom on modesty

'I never knew a person so poised that he wasn't disconcerted when a doorknob came off in his hand.'
—*W.C. Fields*

When we walk close to nature, we come to a better understanding of life; for, it is from the natural world that we first emerged and to which we still belong.

Notes

We don't have to circle the world to find **beauty** and **fulfilment**. After all, most of living has to happen in the mind. To quote an anonymous sage: 'The world is only the size of each man's head.'

Death moves about
at random, without
discriminating between
the innocent and the evil,
the poor and the rich.
The only difference is that
the poor usually handle
it better.

'Whoever boasts himself of
a false gift is like clouds
and wind without rain.'
—*Proverbs 25:14*

·Ruskin Bond·

Follow instinct rather than
intelligence, and it may
result in a modicum
of happiness.

The value of stillness—
while the hands are
busy, the heart cannot
understand!

·A Little Book of Life·

Happiness is as elusive as a butterfly, and you must never pursue it. If you stay very still, it may come and settle on your hand. But only briefly. Savour those moments, for they will not come your way very often.

'Whatever you have, spend less.'
—*Samuel Johnson*

'If you want to make sure that your wife will listen to what you have to say, do your talking in your sleep.'
—*Anonymous*

'Nothing can be loved too much, but all things can be loved in the wrong way.'
—*W.H. Auden*

'I've seen more tears run down the pretty faces than the plain ones.'
—*Evelyn Nesbit*

There is no harm in sitting in an office and making money, but sometimes you must look out of the window. And look at the changing light.

·Ruskin Bond·

'Two things a man can never hide—that he is drunk and that he is in love.'
—*Anonymous*

'If I am not for myself, who will be for me? And if I am not for others, what am I? And if not now, when?'
—*Hillel*

How much time do we spend counting and cataloguing what we possess—people, objects, money? Life usually happens when we stop doing that.

Before you enumerate another's faults, take time to count to ten... ten of your faults.

·Ruskin Bond·

Maxim from my grandmother's recipe book: 'Let not your tongue cut your throat!'

'About the time we think we can make both ends meet, someone goes and moves the ends.'

—*Herbert Hoover*

Napoleon: 'Never awake me when you have good news to announce, because, with good news, nothing presses; but when you have bad news, arouse me immediately, for then there is not an instant to be lost.'

'Insist on yourself; never imitate.'
—*Ralph Waldo Emerson*

There are definite limits
on a man's wisdom, but
absolutely no limits
on his stupidity.

A new thinker or teacher
is often one who does not
know what the old thinkers
have thought.

Notes

We must try to make
the end of the journey
better than the beginning,
as long as we are journeying;
but when we come to the end,
we must be
happy
and
content.

—*Epicurus*

Fame is like the wind.
It blows in all directions,
then vanishes
without warning.

He who laughs with you is
a friend. He who laughs at
you is an enemy.

·Ruskin Bond·

The greatest truths are
full of fiction, the greatest
fiction is full of truths.

A fool always tries to
appear wise. The wise man
is not afraid to play
the clown.

'Success is where preparation and opportunity meet.'
—*Bobby Unser*

The egoist? He's the one who does not think of you.

Contentment is easier to attain than happiness. I take as my guide the small ginger cat who arrives on my terrace every afternoon, to curl up in the sun and slumber peacefully for a couple of hours.

When a man says money can do anything, that settles it. He hasn't any.

Arthur Wellesley: 'Nothing except a battle lost can be half so melancholy as a battle won.'

'No great thing cometh suddenly into being, for not even a bunch of grapes can, or a fig.'

—*Epictetus*

A West Indian proverb:
'Every day no Christmas,
an' every day no rainy day.'

Select wisely the person
you must live with
forever—yourself.

'Come, friend, let us lose tomorrow's grief
And seize this moment of life:
Tomorrow, this ancient inn abandoned,
We shall be equal with those born seven thousand years ago!'
—*Omar Khayyam*

Let this little book be a garden in your pocket.

·Ruskin Bond·